AF327611

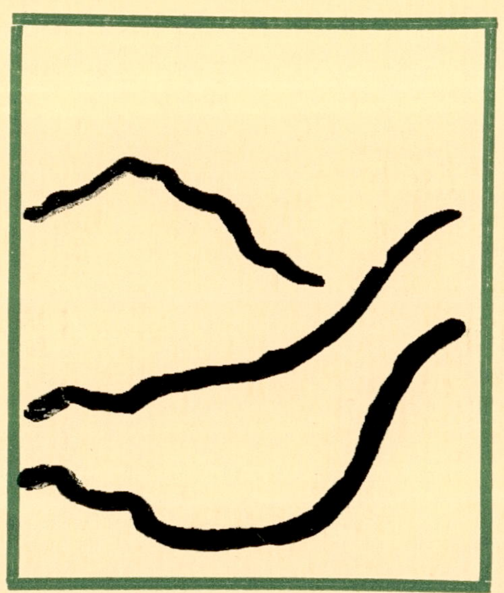

GREEN MOUNTAIN, BLACK MOUNTAIN

Green Mountain Black Mountain

ANNE STEVENSON

The poem will also be published in Anne Stevenson's new collection *Minute by Glass Minute* (Oxford University Press, 1982) and is printed here by permission of Oxford University Press.
All rights reserved.
ISBN 0-937672-07-6
Printed in the United States of America

The author wishes to express her thanks to the Welsh Arts Council for a bursary received in 1981 which enabled her to finish this poem. **Green Mountain, Black Mountain** was first published in the *Michigan Quarterly Review*, Winter 1982, with simultaneous publication in the *Anglo-Welsh Review* in Wales.

Cover art by Vicki Moran
Design by Clarence Wolfshohl

Photo by Susan Butler

Rowan Tree Press
124 Chestnut Street
Boston, Massachusetts 02108

for my parents

I

White pine, sifter of sunlight,
Wintering host in New England woods,
Cold scent, icicle to the nostril,
Path without echo, unmarked page.

    I formed you, you forget me,
    I keep you like a fossil.
    The air is full of footprints.
    Rings of the sycamore spell you.
    Your name spills out on April ground
            with October leafmold . . .

Beechbole, cheekbone of the interior,
Sugaring maple, tap of sour soil,
Woody sweetness, wine of the honeybark,
Mountain trickle, bitter to the tongue,

    You acquired me out of wilderness,
    Grey maples streaked with birches,
    With your black-shuttered
    White wooden house flanked with porches,
    Your black-painted peeling front doors.

Pairs of shuttered windows,
Sheltered lives.
Child's work, the symmetry,
Thin graves for narrow souls.

    Terra there was before *Terra Nova*.
    You brought to my furred hills
    Axes, steeples; your race split
    Hugely on the heave of the Atlantic . . .

In April the earth serves patiently its purpose.
Trees unclench their closed crimson fists

Against return. How many weeks before ease will anull
These dark, matted, snow-beaten scraps of mowin?

> Dry wind-eaten beechleaves
> Flutter under their birth arch.
> Steeplebush and blackberry
> Stoop to beginnings.

Green mountain with its shadow future,
Unwritten days in the buried stone.
Black mountain, colour of roots,
Clay in the roof, gag to the mouth.

II

In border Powys, a landrover
stalls on a hilltrack.
A farmer gets out with a halter,
plods to a tilted field where
a mare and her colt have rolled
the wet soil of Welch weather

all a mud-lashed winter.

Unlatching the gate, he
forces the halter on the caked
anxious head of the mare,
then leads her away to where
a plan of his own makes fast
to some spindle purpose
the fate of the three of them.

The inscrutable movements of the man
puzzle the horses, who
follow him, nevertheless,
up the piebald track,
snowdeep in drift in places,
tyre-churned with red mud.

These are the Black Mountains
where the drenched sleep of Wales
troubles King Arthur in his cave,
where invisible hankerings of the dead
trouble the farms spilled over them --
the heaped fields, graves and tales.

The farmer with his brace of horses
(barker at strangers, inbreeder of races)
is Teyrnon still, or Pryderi the colt-child,
fixed without shape or time
between the ghost-pull of Annwfyn
that other world, underworld, feathering
green Wales in its wold-mist,

and the animal pull of his green dunged boots.
Which take him, as he takes his horses,
up a red and white track for which he has
no name. A habit. An inheritance.
A cold night's work getting lambs born.
And in the morning,   again.

III

Rain in the wind
        and the green need of again
            opening in this Welsh woods.

5

"Vermont" I want to call it,
        "Green Mountain," rafter
                over sleepers in the black

hill of returnings, shadows
        in the dry cave
                of the happened.

At a peal of memory
        they rise in tatters, imperatives,
                the word fossils,

webs of thready handwriting,
        typewritten strata, uncut stones
                culled for the typesetters' cemeteries.

*

If you, mother, had survived
        you would have written . . .

As when we were children
	and everything was going on
		forever in New Haven

you scratched in your journal:
	It is a strange reaction but
	suddenly the war has made it
	imperative to spend time at home
	reading and being with my children.

The pen drew its meanings
	through vacancy,
		threading a history.

*

And what shall I do
	with this touchable page that has
		closed over doubt in her voice these forty years?

I set the words up on the table,
    feeling for continuities,
        tap them with my quick nail. Listen.

But her shell has buried her echo in them.
    It is small, hard, a child's tooth,
        a guilt-pebble, a time preserved like an ammonite.

Then maybe on the second
    or the third day of March
        you overhear a blackbird in a dead elm,

or a thrush singing almost before you wake,
    or you walk unexpectedly into the calm
        ravage of a riverbank

where a broken branch
    kneels into rising water to remake
        predictable green tips,

and I know that it matters
    and does not matter --
        it is you, not I, who lives these things.

*

We'd thought she'd want us, knowing it was cancer,
But when we went to her she winced.
Her hand became a supplicating blur
That winter, and we didn't see her much.
There was a kind of wilting away in her
As if she couldn't bear the human touch
Of voices. Or was it something more
Unkind in us, a wincing helplessness
Or reckless anger? She was dying
At us.   Dying was accusing.

*

IV

After April snow,
such a green thaw.
A chiff-chaff chips a warmer home
in that cloud-cliff.
The river bulges,
flexing brown Japanese muscles,
moving its smooth planes in multitudes.
Threads of white melt stitch
the slashed flanks of the hill fields.

Soon the animal will be well again,
hunting and breeding
in grass-covered bones.
It peers from these clinical windows
apprehensive but healing.
To be whole would be enough.
To be whole and well and warm,
content with a kill.

V

Crossing the Atlantic. That child-pure
impulse of away, retreating
to our God-forgetting present

from the God-rot of old Boston and Leyden.
"To remove to some other place
for sundry weighty and solid reasons."

And then to be the letter of the place,
the page of the Lord's approval, within
the raw green misery of the risk.

"For there they should be liable to
famine and nakedness
and the want, in a manner, of all things."

Without things, then, the thing was to be done,
the mountain changed, the chance
regiven. Taken again.

*

Crossing the Atlantic. Passport,
        briefcase, two trays full of cellophane food
                and a B grade film.

No, father, I mean
        across to the America
                that lives in the film of my mind.

You would have to be
        alive there, distilled
                on the spool of your life,

not as a photograph --
        unhappiness or happiness staring
                from the onceness of a time --

but as the living practice of a now,
        rehearsed as certain habits and expressions --
                your shoulders' loosened stoop to the piano,

or the length of you decanted on a chair,

animate in argument, ash scattered
    from your cigarette like punctuation.

I think of the goodness of the house,
    the companionable presences of cellos
        punished in the corners like children,

or gleaming like the muscle-backs of girls,
    smug in the enslavement of one lover
        or another since the 18th century

made its music bread and water
    for the likes of us who,
        having no other faith,

still kept our covenant with
    foreign Bach, with Schubert
        after-dinner Mozarts, Razumovskis . . .

(The Polish ghettos
    drained into the cattle cars.
        Dying Vienna bled us violins.)

And yet through those

immortal-seeding summers,
        music, that rare mediant window,

was glass through which we grew,
        a grace we had not
            guilt enough to refuse.

*

Chestnut blossom with its crimson stigmata,
Stamen-thrust from confused hands --
Five white petals, multiple in a
Competing order, so that each candelabrum stands
As a tree of defeats around a pieta . . .

To be as one mother in a storm of sons,
The charred faces and cracked skulls of a
Comfortable century. Petal-white sands
Made of tiny shellfish. The crashed motorcycle
Where the sea withdraws with no grief at all.

In dread of the black mountain,
Gratitude for the green mountain.
In dread of the green mountain,
Gratitude for the black mountain.

In dread of the fallen lintel and the ghosted hearth,
    gratitude for the green mountain.
In dread of the crying missile and the jet's chalk,
    gratitude for the black mountain.

In dread of the titled thief, thigh-deep in his name,
    gratitude for the green mountain.
In dread of the neon street to the armed moon,
    gratitude for the black mountain.

In dread of the gilded bible and the rod-cut hand,
    gratitude for the green mountain.
In dread of the uncrossed boards behind the blazing man,
    gratitude for the black mountain.

*

In dread of my shadow on the Green Mountain.
gratitude for this April of the Black Mountain,
as the grass fountains out of its packed roots
and a thrush repeats the repertoire of his threats:

I hate it, I hate it, I hate it.

Go away. Go away.

I will not, I will not, I will not.

Come again. Come again.

Swifts twist on the syllables of the wind currents.

Blackbirds are the cellos of the deep farms.

NOTE

Green Mountain, Black Mountain was written between the spring of 1980, when I returned briefly to the Green Mountains in Vermont, and that of 1981, when I was living among the Black Mountains of Wales. Contrast between the new world (old to me) and the old world (rich in history and myth, but new to me) is the theme of this poem which emerged, finally, as a prolonged elegy to my parents. My father, Charles Stevenson, was a pianist before he was a philosopher, and I remember him so much more clearly as a musician than as an academic that I have tried to write this poem as the *cantata* I would have written for him had I been able to write music. I have felt the sections to be arias, recitatives, chorales; following an introductory incantation, but it would be an unnecessary affectation, I think, to label them as such.

In Section II, which takes place in Wales, *Teyrnon* and *Pryderi* are mythological characters who appear in the first branch of *The Mabinogian. Annwfyn* is the Welsh equivalent of *Sidh* in Irish, home of the Tuatha de Dannan.

In Section V I have borrowed from William Bradford's *History of Plymouth Plantation* as quoted in Perry Miller's *The American Puritans* (New York, 1956).

Section III is dedicated to my mother, Louise Destler Stevenson, to whom I owe more than I can express. A spirit of sensibility, generosity and intelligence, she was a greater human being than she was a writer, and with her death almost all of her was lost. In the final section, the chant of the thrush imitates the various tunes of the British Song Thrush; blackbirds in Britain are lowvoiced, melancholy, exquisite.

The Rowan Tree, or Wiggen, or Witchen, venerated
by the Druids, grows in both Wales and Vermont.
The Welsh name is Cerddinen; in Vermont it is called
the Mountain Ash.

———

This book was set in Modern Roman by Clarence
Wolfshohl at Timberline Press, Fulton, Missouri.

The text printed on Kilmory India; cover on
Kilmory Moss.

———

Poetry Pamphlet No. 1

Rowan Tree Press
124 Chestnut Street
Boston, Massachusetts 02108

A